BE AN ELEVATOR MECHANIC

GUIDE TO THE TRADES

D0001758

Published in the United States of America by Cherry Lake Publishing
Ann Arbor, Michigan
www.cherrylakepublishing.com

Reading Adviser: Marla Conn, MS, Ed., Literacy specialist, Read-Ability, Inc.

Photo Credits: Cover and pages 1, 6, and 26, ©Dmitry Kalinovsky/Shutterstock; page 5, ©Dragon Images/Shutterstock;
page 8, ©coloritmail/Shutterstock; page 10, ©milan2099/iStockphoto.com; page 13, ©Monkey Business Images/Shutterstock;
page 14, ©Creative Stock Studio/Shutterstock; page 16, ©KlingSup/Shutterstock; page 19, ©thanatphoto/Shutterstock; page 20,
©Rachid Jalayanadeja/Shutterstock; page 22, ©vgajic/iStockphoto.com; page 25, ©xfilephotos/Shutterstock; page 28,
©Dmitri Ma/Shutterstock

Copyright ©2020 by Cherry Lake Publishing
All rights reserved. No part of this book may be reproduced or utilized in
any form or by any means without written permission from the publisher.

Library of Congress Cataloging-in-Publication Data has been filed and is available
at catalog.loc.gov

Cherry Lake Publishing would like to acknowledge the work of The Partnership for 21st Century Learning.
Please visit *www.p21.org* for more information.

Printed in the United States of America
Corporate Graphics

ABOUT THE AUTHOR

Wil Mara is the author of over 175 fiction and nonfiction books for children. He has written
many titles for Cherry Lake Publishing, including the popular *Global Citizens: Modern Media*
and *Citizen's Guide* series. More about his work can be found at www.wilmara.com.

TABLE OF CONTENTS

CHAPTER 1

Keeping Things Moving 4

CHAPTER 2

Becoming an Elevator Mechanic 12

CHAPTER 3

On the Job 18

CHAPTER 4

Legal Considerations 24

THINK ABOUT IT 30
FIND OUT MORE.. 31
GLOSSARY 32
INDEX 32

Keeping Things Moving

Vicky Tanaka wakes up as her alarm clock rings at 6:00 a.m., just as it does every weekday morning. After a quick shower, she dresses in her usual work clothes—a pair of navy blue pants and a matching shirt. Stitched into the shirt above the pocket is a patch that reads "Gibson Elevator Repair Service." Gibson is one of the oldest elevator-service companies in Vicky's area. She has worked for the company for more than 20 years. Because Vicky lives in Texas, a state with many people and tall buildings, there are always plenty of elevators to work on. Thousands of people in the state are employed as elevator mechanics.

Without elevators, getting to the upper floors of tall buildings would be difficult and time-consuming.

Vicky goes into the kitchen and has breakfast, then heads out to her car. She starts it up and gets on the road. Twenty minutes later, she pulls into the Gibson parking lot. Inside the main building, she meets with her boss to discuss the day's work schedule. Then she heads back out to the parking lot to get into a different vehicle—one of the company vans. The van has the Gibson logo on the side, along with the company's phone number and web address. In the back of the van are all

Elevator mechanics sometimes work in tight spaces.

the tools, replacement parts, and other things she will need during the course of the day.

Vicky pulls out of the lot and heads toward her first job of the day, which is at an office complex downtown. As she's sitting in light morning traffic, she thinks about how much she enjoys driving to different job **sites** each day. She doesn't have to work in the same place all the time. The time she spends on the road gives her time to think and clear her mind between jobs. And because she goes to so many different places, she never gets bored with her surroundings.

Just before 7:30, Vicky arrives at the office complex. As soon as she gets out of the van, she starts looking at the building through the eyes of an elevator mechanic. She notices that it has five floors and is not that old. That's great, she thinks, because it means the elevator system should still be in good shape.

21st Century Content

There are roughly 22,100 elevator mechanics employed in the United States. These workers are more common in some areas than others. The states that employ the most elevator mechanics are listed here:

- New York: 4,510
- Texas: 2,960
- Florida: 1,930
- Maryland: 1,680
- California: 1,630

Bearings come in a wide variety of shapes and sizes, and they are used in many different mechanical devices.

Gibson has a service contract with the company that owns the office building. That means the company is fully responsible for maintaining the elevator systems here. Today, Vicky needs to run a routine check to make sure the building's elevators are running correctly. She goes inside and unlocks the door that leads to the elevator maintenance area. This is a behind-the-scenes place that most people never see. Vicky has gotten used to the fascinating sights in rooms like these. There is a big rectangular box known as an elevator car and the tall shaft that the car travels through. There are steel cables that pull the car up or guide it down, as well as the motor system that supplies the power to make all this happen.

Vicky has a checklist, and she needs to go through it one item at a time. She starts by making sure the elevator car travels between floors at the proper speed. She checks to see if it stops and starts smoothly and stays **level** as it moves. Are all the lights inside the car working? Do the doors open and close without any trouble? Are all the safety features functioning correctly? She needs to check all of these things and many more.

At one point, Vicky notices that one of the **bearings** is making noise. A bearing looks like a small steel wheel. It has rollers sealed inside to help it spin smoothly. There are many bearings within the mechanical parts of the elevator system. Through her many years of experience, Vicky knows that a noisy bearing is an early sign of trouble. She locates the bearing in question and makes a note on the maintenance report to come back and replace it within the next two weeks.

Working as an elevator mechanic can be a very satisfying and rewarding job.

Vicky is done with this first service call at 9:30. She goes back to the van and sets off toward the next site, a shopping mall on the other side of town. There, she will need to figure out why one of the elevators has stopped working. As she drives, she thinks about what her job really means—making sure elevators are safe for people to ride. Every day, hundreds or maybe even thousands of people step onto elevators that Vicky has repaired. Knowing that her work is helping to keep these people safe is one of the most rewarding parts of her job.

CHAPTER 2

Becoming an Elevator Mechanic

Elevators are complex machines. They are packed with computers, moving parts, and other technology. Understanding every detail of how an elevator works is essential to being a good mechanic. This means all elevator mechanics must be well educated before they start their careers.

The path to becoming an elevator mechanic typically begins in high school. Future mechanics should pay particular attention in math class. Math skills will be an important part of their eventual on-the-job duties. Shop or mechanics classes will be useful, too. Learning how different machines function will help students develop an ability to find and fix mechanical problems. Science courses, especially physics, will also be useful

Learning about robotics or other mechanical devices will provide knowledge and skills that will be useful to any elevator mechanic.

to future elevator mechanics. Learning why and how things move will help them understand what makes elevators work.

Following high school, a future elevator mechanic has several choices. One possibility is to attend a vocational school or trade school that offers courses in elevator repair. The more common option is to seek an **apprenticeship**. An apprenticeship is an on-the-job program where a student learns from a **mentor**. The mentor is a professional, working mechanic with many years of experience.

In exchange for sharing their knowledge with apprentices, mentors get an extra set of hands to help out with tough jobs.

Apprenticeships can usually be found through a local **union**. A union is an organization that protects the interests of professionals in a certain trade, such as plumbers, electricians, carpenters, or elevator mechanics. The union will interview apprenticeship applicants and decide who is best suited for joining the profession.

Most learning during an apprenticeship comes in the form of hands-on experience. Students will learn about elevator installation, repair, troubleshooting, and maintenance by doing it themselves on real job sites. As they work, their mentors will observe and provide advice and feedback as necessary. Apprentices benefit by this guidance and supervision—they don't have to worry about causing problems by making mistakes as they learn.

Apprentices will become familiar with all the tools of the trade. These include common hand tools such as hammers, wrenches, and pliers. Power tools such as drills, saws, grinders, blowtorches, and welders are useful as well. Elevator mechanics also rely on more specialized tools, such as devices that measure the flow of electricity.

There is usually some classroom learning involved in an apprenticeship. Apprentices will study different kinds of elevator systems and learn about topics such as electrical systems and fire safety.

Working with elevators also requires knowledge of specialized computer software. For example, there are programs that are designed to communicate with the computer systems of the elevators themselves. When trying to figure out what is wrong with an elevator, a mechanic might use a tablet computer to connect with the elevator's computer "brain." Learning how to

During their apprenticeships, mechanics learn how to repair many different kinds of elevator systems.

use this software is an important part of the classroom instruction an apprentice receives.

The normal length of an elevator mechanic apprenticeship is about four years. Each year of the program requires around 144 hours of instruction and about 2,000 hours of paid on-the-job training. Upon completion, the apprentice is usually required to pass tests, both written and hands-on, to prove their abilities and knowledge. Passing these tests will allow them to become certified elevator mechanics and begin their careers. In apprenticeships that are arranged through a union, newly certified mechanics remain members of that union. The union then arranges employment for them.

Once a young elevator mechanic gets a little experience, the pay for this kind of work can be very good. Someone in this field can expect to make around $80,000 per year, which is above average for a job in the trades.

Life and Career Skills

There are different specialties within the field of elevator repair and maintenance. An elevator installer focuses on putting in new elevator systems from scratch. This is more of a construction profession. Installers need to know how to read and understand **blueprints** and select the best equipment for the job. Then they assemble everything and finally test the system to ensure it is working.

Repair and maintenance mechanics take care of existing elevator systems. Their duties include routine checkups, which are usually performed annually. They also address problems that have already occurred, including emergency situations.

Some mechanics specialize in elevators used for specific tasks, such as freight elevators. These systems are designed to haul very heavy loads. Therefore, they are designed more for strength than speed.

CHAPTER 3

On the Job

A career as an elevator mechanic can be very rewarding. Mechanics who really know what they're doing are in very high demand. This means they can look forward to decent pay and steady employment. Working as a mechanic is not easy, though. The day-to-day duties of an elevator mechanic offer numerous challenges. The work itself can be divided into two broad categories—installation of new elevator systems, and maintenance and repair of existing systems. Each requires a special set of learned skills. Certain natural personality traits will also make some people better suited to the job than others.

Perhaps the most important thing any mechanic needs is an eye for detail. Being able to notice small problems can help them

Elevator mechanics learn to observe even the smallest details about how an elevator is running. This helps them correctly identify and solve problems.

predict bigger problems that could occur later without maintenance. A good mechanic will notice when an elevator car moves in a way that isn't quite right or when the elevator makes a slightly strange sound.

Analytical thinking and problem-solving skills are also essential. Elevator mechanics will face unexpected issues every day. They need to remain calm and follow the commonsense steps that go with finding a solution. The process of troubleshooting, for example, begins with diagnosing a

Safety harnesses are attached to sturdy surfaces using hooks and clips. If a mechanic slips, the harness will prevent them from falling down an elevator shaft.

problem. This requires using various testing equipment to check brakes, motors, switches, and control systems to locate the source of the problem. Once that's completed, the mechanic has to find the faulty part and adjust or replace it. This can be a painstaking process.

An elevator mechanic also needs a wide variety of mechanical skills. Elevators contain many different systems. There are machines to physically lift and lower the elevator car. There are electrical systems to control these machines.

[21ST CENTURY SKILLS LIBRARY]

In modern elevators, there are many computers. On one day, a mechanic may be doing work similar to that of a plumber, such as cutting and welding the pipes required for the flow of **hydraulic** fluid. On another day, the mechanic might be

Life and Career Skills

As with any job in the building trades, there are safety risks involved with working on elevators. Thankfully, many of these risks can be greatly reduced using the right safety equipment and procedures.

Elevator mechanics—particularly those who specialize in installation—spend a fair share of time in high places. That means falls are always a risk. Mechanics typically wear a full-body safety vest with an attached harness when working high above the ground. A helmet should always be used as well, since parts and loose tools can fall from high places if someone makes a mistake.

Many of the parts within an elevator system are electrified and can become very hot during the course of ordinary operation. Mechanics often wear protective clothing, gloves, and eyewear. This helps them avoid burns and shocks as they work.

A strong knowledge of electronics is essential for any elevator mechanic.

dealing with an elevator's electrical wiring. Anyone who's ever been on an elevator has seen all the buttons on the car's control panel. Behind this panel is a dizzying array of multicolored wires running in all directions. Working with these kinds of systems is normally the job of an electrician. But an elevator mechanic has to be skilled in that area, too.

Elevator mechanics also need to be self-sufficient. They often spend a good deal of their work time on their own. Most general repair and maintenance jobs can usually be handled by one person. For example, a maintenance checklist for the inside of an elevator car might include examining the interior for damage and replacing any indicator lights that are faulty or have burned out. After that, the mechanic might test the motion of the car, to make sure stops and starts are smooth and that the ride itself is level and steady. They check to see that the doors open and close at a normal speed and that the sensors controlling the door restrictors are operating properly. All of these tasks can easily be handled by a single mechanic.

For the most part, the only time an elevator mechanic works with others is during new construction and installation. In such events, communication skills are crucial. Elevator installation projects can take anywhere from a few weeks to a few months. This means the mechanics working on the project will have to spend a lot of time around each other and rely on each other to complete their job.

CHAPTER 4

Legal Considerations

Countless people rely on elevators every day to get to and from their jobs and homes. These people need to be able to trust that the elevators they use will be safe and reliable. As a result, there are many laws and regulations in place to help make sure elevators are always installed correctly and properly maintained. Many of these rules have direct effects on an elevator mechanic's job.

For example, elevator mechanics are often required to be **licensed**. Licensing is a state government's way of verifying that a mechanic is skilled and knowledgeable enough to work with elevators.

The mechanical devices that raise and lower elevator cars are typically located in special rooms out of sight of most people who ride elevators.

Currently, 35 U.S. states require elevator mechanics to get licensed before they can work legally. While the others do not yet require a license to work, this could change in the future as new laws are passed. Mechanics who live in states that require a license must start by filling out an application. Then they must pass the state's tests to prove that they are able to do the job. Such tests often feature both written and hands-on sections. Those who pass are rewarded with a license that is

Installing a new elevator might involve welding pieces of metal together.

good for a certain period of time, such as two years. After that time is up, a mechanic must once again pass the test to earn a new license.

It's important to note that a licensing test will not be the same each time. Technologies and techniques change over time, and elevator mechanics are expected to keep up with such developments. Some mechanics might enroll in career development classes throughout their careers to learn about new advancements in their field. Others might simply stay up-to-date by reading journals or other publications relating to elevator technology.

A big part of becoming licensed involves learning about local building **codes**. Building codes are a set of rules that detail how buildings can be constructed and maintained. For

21st Century Content

The need for elevator mechanics is growing at a faster-than-average pace. According to the U.S. Bureau of Labor Statistics, the current annual growth rate is about 12 percent. In 2018, there were roughly 22,100 elevator mechanic jobs in the United States, and around 2,700 more are expected to be added within the next 10 years. This means there should be plenty of job opportunities for people who want to become elevator mechanics in the coming years.

The great majority of jobs in this field—about 90 percent—come from building equipment **contractors**. Another 3 percent of jobs come from the government. Just 1 percent or so come from educational services.

Thanks to elevator mechanics, people don't usually need to think about whether or not an elevator is going to work. They simply press a button.

example, a new elevator has to meet certain safety standards. It might be required to handle a certain amount of weight or be equipped with specific safety features. Mechanics are required to know all the current building codes related to elevators.

Codes can also affect the routine maintenance that is carried out by elevator mechanics. Part of the mechanic's job is to check whether the elevators are up to code. If they are not, problems will need to be addressed fairly quickly. In many places, code violations have to be resolved within 30 days, or else the elevator systems may be shut down and the building owners subject to fines. If this happens, the building owners could take legal action against the service company they hired to keep the elevators maintained.

Reputable elevator service companies also make sure they are **bonded**. This means they have insurance that covers any problems that might occur as a result of their work. For example, if a mechanic makes a mistake and causes damage to an elevator or some other feature of a building while working, the repair costs will be covered by the insurance. Bonds can also cover personal injuries caused by improperly maintained elevators. It should be noted, however, that elevator service companies that rely on bonds to cover their mistakes will have increasing difficulty securing another policy following each incident. So while a bond helps protect an elevator service company from financial losses, it is better not to have to use it.

Think About It

The earliest known elevator-like device was built by the mathematician Archimedes sometime around 236 BCE. It worked using a system of pulleys and was powered by human strength. Steam-powered passenger elevators were in operation by the late 1700s, and they became even more common in the mid-1800s during the rise of American industry. Coal miners, for example, used elevator-like lifts to bring themselves and their equipment through the mine shafts. Many of these early elevators were notoriously unsafe. It wasn't until 1852 when a man named Elisha Otis invented the safety elevator, which prevented the car from falling if the cable broke. How do you think people got from floor to floor before elevators were common? How have elevators changed over time?

If you became an elevator mechanic, which specialty do you think you'd choose? What parts of the job do you think you'd like best and least? Explain your answers.

Find Out More

BOOKS

Labrecque, Ellen. *Electrician*. Ann Arbor, MI: Cherry Lake Publishing, 2017.

Maurer, Tracy. *Elevators*. Vero Beach, FL: Rourke Educational Media, 2017.

Rhatigan, Joe. *Get a Job at the Construction Site*. Ann Arbor, MI: Cherry Lake Publishing, 2017.

WEBSITES

Time: This Is the Patent for the Device That Made Elevators a Lot Less Dangerous
http://time.com/4700084/elevator-patent-history-otis-safety
Learn more about inventor Elisha Otis and his remarkable design for the first safety elevator.

U.S. Bureau of Labor Statistics—Occupational Outlook Handbook: Elevator Installers and Repairers
https://www.bls.gov/ooh/construction-and-extraction/elevator-installers-and-repairers.htm
Learn how to become an elevator mechanic and find out more about the profession at this government site.

GLOSSARY

apprenticeship (uh-PREN-tis-ship) training situation in which someone learns a skill by working with an expert on the job

bearings (BAIR-ingz) machine parts that reduce friction between other moving parts

blueprints (BLOO-printz) drawings that illustrate how a structure needs to be built

bonded (BAHND-id) having an insurance policy to cover damages caused by a worker while on the job

codes (KOHDZ) rules that determine the correct design and construction of buildings

contractors (KAHN-trak-turz) people who hire others to do work

hydraulic (hye-DRAW-lik) relating to machines that are powered by the movement of liquids

level (LEV-uhl) having a flat, even, horizontal surface

licensed (LYE-suhnsd) certified by a state to assure that someone is qualified to perform a job

mentor (MEN-tor) someone who teaches a less experienced person

sites (SITES) locations of jobs

union (YOON-yuhn) an organization that protects the interests of a certain type of worker, such as an elevator mechanic

INDEX

apprenticeships, 13–16, 17

bearings, 9
blueprints, 17
bonding, 29
building codes, 27–29

cables, 9
certification, 16–17
checklists, 9, 23
checkups, 8, 9, 17, 23
clothing, 4, 21
communication, 23
computers, 15, 21
contractors, 27

details, 18–19

education, 12–16, 26–27
electrical systems, 15, 20, 21, 22

elevator cars, 8, 9, 19, 20, 22, 23
elevator shafts, 8–9
employment, 4, 7, 17, 27

freight elevators, 17

injuries, 29
installation, 14, 17, 18, 21, 23, 24
installers, 17

job sites, 6, 7, 11, 15

licensing, 24–27

maintenance, 8, 14, 17, 18, 19, 22, 23, 24, 27, 28, 29
mechanical skills, 12, 20–21
mentors, 13, 15
motor systems, 9, 20

personalities, 18
problem solving, 12, 19–20

regulations, 24, 25, 28
repairs, 17, 18

safety, 11, 15, 21, 24, 28
salary, 17
self-sufficiency, 22–23
service contracts, 8, 29
software, 15–16

tests, 16, 25, 26
tools, 5–6, 15, 21

unions, 14, 17

workdays, 4, 5–9, 11, 18, 19, 21–22